Swimming with Sharks

Bull Sharks

CHRISTINE THOMAS ALDERMAN

BLACK
RABBIT
BOOKS

BOLT

Bolt is published by Black Rabbit Books
P.O. Box 3263, Mankato, Minnesota, 56002.
www.blackrabbitbooks.com
Copyright © 2020 Black Rabbit Books

Marysa Storm, editor; Grant Gould, designer;
Omay Ayres, photo researcher

Library of Congress Cataloging-in-Publication Data
Names: Alderman, Christine Thomas, author.
Title: Bull sharks / by Christine Thomas Alderman.
Description: Mankato, Minnesota : Black Rabbit Books, [2020] |
Series: Bolt. Swimming with sharks | Audience: Age 8-12. | Audience:
Grade 4 to 6. | Includes bibliographical references and index.
Identifiers: LCCN 2018036387 (print) | LCCN 2018037369 (ebook) |
ISBN 9781680728675 (e-book) | ISBN 9781680728613 (library binding) |
ISBN 9781644660461 (paperback)
Subjects: LCSH: Bull shark–Juvenile literature.
Classification: LCC QL638.95.C3 (ebook) | LCC QL638.95.C3 A43 2020
(print) | DDC 597.3/4–dc23
LC record available at https://lccn.loc.gov/2018036387

Printed in the United States. 1/19

Image Credits
Alamy: Ben Horton, 4–5; BlueOrang-
eStudio, 18 (top turtle, bkgd); David Fleeth-
am, 28; MARK CONLIN / VWPICS, 11; Media
Drum World, 18 (btm); Michael Patrick O'Neill, Cover,
18 (shark), 28–29; awionline.org: Animal Welfare Institute,
25; Getty: Alexander Safonov, 6, 17; iStock: ShaneGross,
26 (top bull), 31; mauioceancenter.com: Maui Ocean Center,
26 (pup); Newscom: Hal Beral Visual&Written, 21; Open Lens:
Lukasz Koncraciuk, 22; seapics.com: Doug Perrine, 29; sketchfab.
com: rstr_tv, 8–9; Shutterstock: AquariusPhotography, 14; Arch-
Man, 3; Ecaterina Sciuchina, 12–13; frantisekhojdysz, 26 (tiger
shark); Jiang Zhongyan, 26 (squid); leonp, 6–7; Luiz Felipe V.
Punte, 1; Maquiladora, 23; Michael Kraus, 26 (fish); Rich Carey,
26 (turtle); robertzwinchell, 14–15; Shane Gross, 32; Willyam
Bradberry, 26 (btm bull)
Every effort has been made to contact copyright
holders for material reproduced in this book. Any
omissions will be rectified in subsequent
printings if notice is given to the
publisher.

Contents

CHAPTER 1

Swimming Along

Sun warms a beach. Dolphins swim and splash in the ocean. Everything seems peaceful. But a blue-gray shark swims close to the shore. The shark matches the sandy, **murky** ocean. It's hard to see. This shadowy shark is a bull shark. It won't hide long. It's hungry, and almost anything will do.

WEIGHT

200 TO 500 POUNDS

(91 to 227 kilograms)

Mess with the Bull and Get the Teeth

Bull sharks are powerful predators. Like bulls on land, they're fast. They're also big and **aggressive**. These fearsome sharks attack with force. They seem to fly through the water.

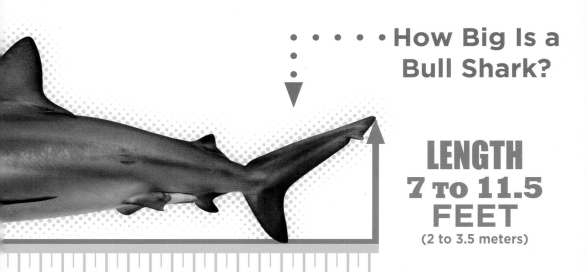

How Big Is a Bull Shark?

LENGTH
7 TO 11.5 FEET
(2 to 3.5 meters)

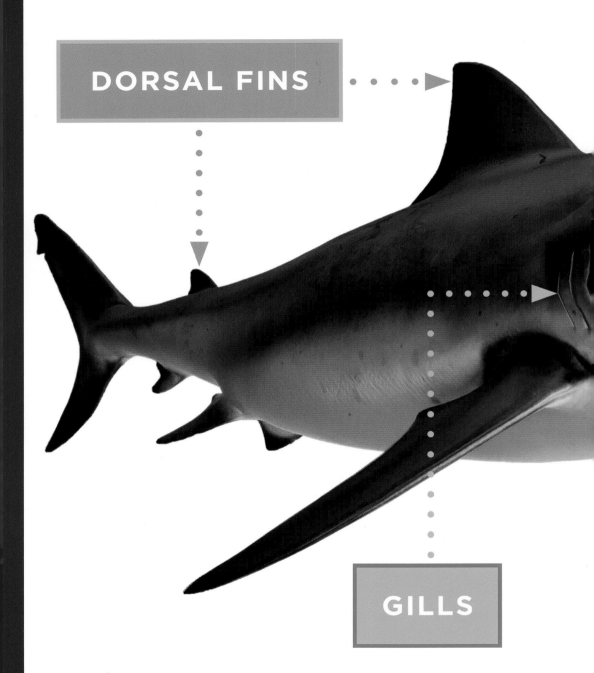

DORSAL FINS

GILLS

SMALL EYES

SNOUT

SERRATED TEETH

THICK BODY

9

CHAPTER 2

Where They Live
and
What They Eat

Bull sharks often swim in shallow **coastal** water. But they don't just live in oceans. They swim in fresh water too. They don't need salt water to survive. Any water is fair game to a bull shark. In fact, they've been found in the Mississippi and Amazon rivers.

Where in the Water?

Different types of sharks swim at different depths in the water.

feet below surface	BULL SHARK	GREAT WHITE SHARK	HAMMERHEAD SHARK	GOBLIN SHARK
0				
1,000				
2,000	surface to 492 feet (150 m)	surface to more than 820 feet (250 m)	surface to about 902 feet (275 m)	131 to 4,265 feet (40 to 1,300 m)
3,000				
4,000				
5,000				

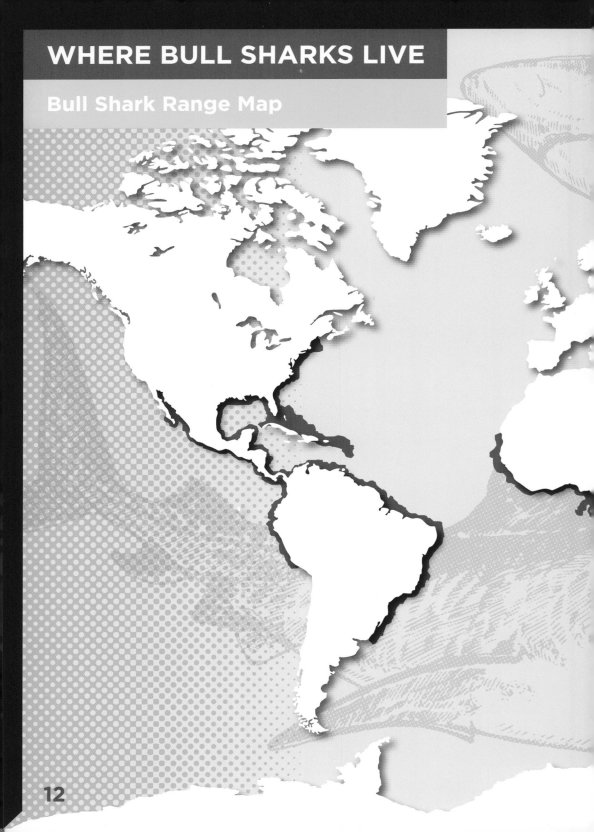

13

Bull, great white, and tiger sharks are most likely to attack people. Shark attacks are still very rare, though. A person is more likely to be struck by lightning.

Dinnertime

Bull sharks swim just about everywhere. And they eat just about everything. Bull sharks feed on fish. These sharks also snatch up squid and stingrays. They snack on shrimp and crabs too. Even birds aren't safe!

Eating Machines

Bull sharks are built to munch. Their teeth act like steak knives. They use them to tear **prey** apart. Bulls' strong jaws help them bite through turtle shells and other tough materials. Their size lets them attack large prey, such as dolphins.

Female bull sharks grow larger than males.

BUMP

BITE

18

Charge!

When hunting, bull sharks don't bite right away. First, they bump prey and swim away. Then they rush back and attack. Scientists call this action a bump and bite.

When bull sharks attack, they pack a punch. They can swim more than 12 miles (19 kilometers) per hour.

Bulls can't see well. The sharks also swim in murky water. Scientists think they bump first to see if something feels like dinner.

CHAPTER 3

Family Life

Bull sharks like their space. Some meet up during **feeding frenzies**. But they often live and hunt alone. Most only meet to **mate**.

Bull sharks usually mate when the water warms up in the summer. Bulls that live in places that are always warm mate year-round.

COMPARING SIZES

Bull Babies

Pregnant bull sharks often swim to fresh water to have pups. Pups are born live. Their mothers don't care for them. But the fresh water keeps them safe. Sharks that need salty water can't come and eat them. Young bull sharks stay in these areas for a while. They leave once they're big enough to handle open water.

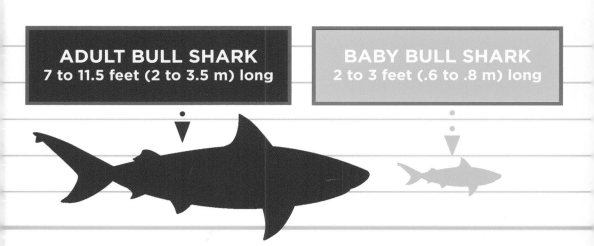

ADULT BULL SHARK
7 to 11.5 feet (2 to 3.5 m) long

BABY BULL SHARK
2 to 3 feet (.6 to .8 m) long

CHAPTER 4

Keeping Sharks Safe

Bull sharks sit at the top of the food chain. Tiger sharks eat young bulls. So do adult bull sharks. But few animals go after adults.

Humans are a threat to bull sharks of all sizes, though. They fish them for their meat, skin, and **oil**. Humans also destroy bulls' freshwater **habitats**.

Bull Shark Food Chain

This food chain shows what eats bull sharks.
It also shows what bull sharks eat.

TIGER SHARKS

ADULT BULL SHARKS

BULL SHARK PUPS

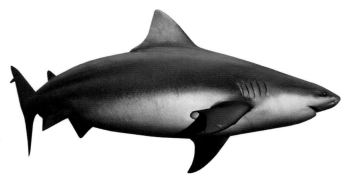

ADULT BULL SHARKS

SEA TURTLES

SQUID

FISH

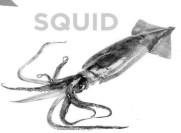

Save the Sharks

Bull sharks need respect and care. It's up to humans to keep their habitats safe and clean. If people aren't careful, these amazing sharks might someday disappear.

Bull shark populations are shrinking. They could soon become endangered.

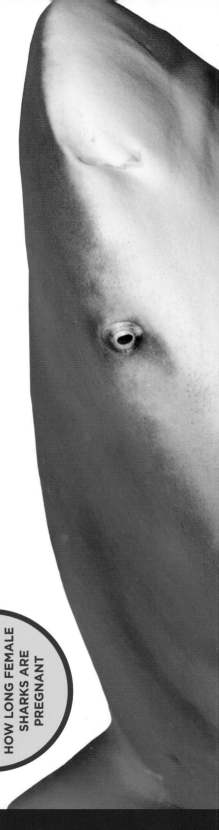

10

TOTAL NUMBER OF GILLS

By the Numbers

16 YEARS
AVERAGE LIFE SPAN

10 to 11 MONTHS
HOW LONG FEMALE SHARKS ARE PREGNANT

up to 13

HOW MANY PUPS
A FEMALE BULL
SHARK CAN HAVE
AT ONE TIME

2,500 miles
(4,023 km)

HOW FAR BULL SHARKS
SWAM UP THE AMAZON RIVER

aggressive (uh-GRES-iv)—showing a readiness to fight, argue, or attack

coastal (KOHS-tl)—near the shore

endangered (in-DAYN-jurd)—close to becoming extinct

feeding frenzy (FEE-ding FREN-zee)— a state of wild activity in which the animals in a group are all trying to eat something

habitat (HAB-uh-tat)—the place where a plant or animal grows or lives

mate (MAYT)—to join together to produce young

murky (MUR-kee)—not clear

oil (OYL)—a greasy liquid substance

pregnant (PREG-nuhnt)—carrying one or more unborn offspring in the body

prey (PRAY)—an animal hunted or killed for food

serrated (SER-ey-tid)—notched or toothed on the edge

BOOKS

Niver, Heather M. Moore. *Bull Sharks After Dark.* Animals of the Night. New York: Enslow Publishing, 2017.

Roseborough, Elizabeth. *Bull Sharks.* The Amazing World of Sharks. Broomall, PA: Mason Crest, 2019.

Waxman, Laura Hamilton. *Bull Sharks.* Sharks. Mankato, MN: Amicus High Interest, Amicus Ink, 2017.

WEBSITES

Bull Shark
kids.nationalgeographic.com/animals/bull-shark/#bull-shark-swimming-ocean-floor1.jpg

Bull Shark
oceana.org/marine-life/sharks-rays/bull-shark

Bull Shark
www.nwf.org/Educational-Resources/Wildlife-Guide/Fish/Bull-Shark

INDEX